WE THE PEOPLE

Democracy As A System

A Humanistic Philosophy of the Future Society
Why a New America Is Necessary
A Guide For Those Who Strive For A Just and Fair Society

REZA REZAZADEH

B.S.M.E., LL.B., J.D., LL.M., Ph.D., S.J.D.

PUBLISH AMERICA

PublishAmerica
Baltimore

First printing

PublishAmerica has allowed this work to remain exactly as the author intended, verbatim, without editorial input.

Hardcover 978-1-4512-3673-6
Softcover 978-1-4512-3672-9
PUBLISHED BY PUBLISHAMERICA, LLLP
www.publishamerica.com
Baltimore

Printed in the United States of America

REZA REZAZADEH
B.S.M.E., LL.B., J.D., LL.M., Ph.D., S.J.D.

Specialized Fields

Technology; Political Science; Economics; American, Continental, Islamic, and International Law

Professor Emeritus, Fulbright Scholar
University of Wisconsin System
Website: www.democracywhere.com
Articles: www.ezinearticles.com/?expert=Dr._Reza_Rezazadeh

To those in the search of a meaning to material and spiritual life; to those aspiring for a just and democratic society; to those exploited, subjugated, alienated, made homeless, victims of poverty and injustice, this work is dedicated.

TABLE OF CONTENTS

INTRODUCTION

The following essay is a simplified presentation of a somehow complex **scientific theory of a technological democratic society**. It is attempted for general public so that the basic idea of the theory could be understood easily, if not profoundly. in its totality. Writing anything scientifically about a society is a complex, arduous, and painstaking task since it requires a vast amount of knowledge in many different fields comprising the structure and operation of the society encompassing all economic, political, social, cultural and technological aspects of life. This is a new and unique theory of democracy never presented before by any thinker, likely because it required a broad knowledge in many different fields not desired at the era of specialization, and the societal life was not as complex as it has gradually become during the last five decades. Two rapidly developing phenomena have been the cause of this complexity, making the existing societal order outmoded, antiquated and impossible of being repaired through reforms.

The first has been the rapid and incredible concentration of wealth and ensuing power in the hands of a small elite who, through huge corporate institutions and friendly governments, have acquired the control of the national economies, now extended to a global scale. The second has been the exponential development in the area of technology, particularly during the last ten years, bringing nearly a total transformation in the way we as the people live and operate, and our societal institutions function.

The most important characteristic of this theory is that it is pragmatic and practical. Karl Marx, the great thinker of the 19th century, spent all his life in formulating a theory of perfect democratic society. Scientifically, he was finally successful. Everyone would work to the best of his or her ability, the products would belong to the community, and everyone would take from it according to his or her needs. However, it could not be materialized because it was a utopian theory of a perfect society, scientifically correct but functionally impossible. The scientific foundation of the theory presented here is very simple; only one principle governs all societal functions and that is **equality of opportunity**. As it will be seen, **technology** is the major component in materializing this principle. The operation of economy is totally privatized and totally controlled by the **working class**, a class of all working people including chief executives, managers and professionals. The national government has nearly no domestic line functions, state governments power is substantially reduced, local government and the private sector manage most of the public functions. More likely, readers may have questions in understanding some aspects of the theory, such as individual rights and freedoms as well as operation of the economic, political, and social aspects of this new system, They will find the answer and clarification for their questions in the three books on the subject written by the author, cited at the end of this writing.

With all difficulties people are facing in developed and developing countries, mainly caused by the capitalistic operation of economy, such as corruption, dishonesty, poverty, lack of health care and education, exploitation, discrimination, unemployment, and many more, this theory of democracy should be looked upon with excitement and hope. All over the world, particularly in advanced countries, people, increasingly conscious of the destructive nature of capitalism, are looking for such a system. Now, here it is a theory of work, comfort, happiness and leisure. It has taken over thirty years of hard work, research, and original thinking .It remains for the people to study, learn, and discuss it, organize for it, and take action to materialize it.

Fortunately, today the situation is very different from any other time in history. We live in an extremely **interconnected** world. What goes on in one place is known instantly in the rest of the world. For those desiring change for the better, this should be taken as a very welcome occasion. It is already being used quite successfully by some organizations even individuals in seeking justice and fairness in as far away places as the remote jungles of Amazons. For example, if I place this essay in my website, instantly its content will be available through Internet to people all over the world. This work is intended to be published in hard cover for those who desire to have a copy in their personal library for their children and the future generation. The electronic information and communication system makes the creation of a movement for action much easier and faster. I hope many proponents of this theory of sweeping change, will initiate such electronic action, keep in constant contact and exchange of ideas with one another and create a strong movement of **We the People** to materialize a just and fair society.

If democracy as a system is established in any country, regardless of its size, even for experimental purpose, its benefits will be immediately witnessed, it will rapidly spread to other countries even those at developing stage. The global instant information and communication system, is a device extremely helpful in creation of any movement even revolution, particularly if the purpose is to bring equality of opportunity, justice and fairness to the people in their daily life. Because of this extraordinary opportunity for success, it seems essential, by employing this system, to create a movement and keep it going. The tools for advancement are all at hand. Once we learn the nature of technological democracy, we know exactly what kind of society we want; we know its exact structure and function; and we know how to start and sustain a peaceful transition until the goal is attained. Only thing needed is a unified movement to put it into action. There should be no doubt that **We the People** together can achieve anything, anyway, and anywhere we desire.

Since governments in advanced countries, under the influence of the economic elite, have established a strong control system through the military, police, secret agents and intelligence departments, violent uprising has no chance of success. Any action must be through peaceful means. The best and easiest way, historically proven and assured of success, is through the application of the myth of **general strike**, formulated and advocated by the French philosopher George Sorel (1847-1922). Here is a brief explanation of the concept; but those who intend to be active in its implementation need to learn more about this extremely effective theory.

Although, late in 19th century, the Marxist socialism was the dominant working class ideology, syndicalism was widely preferred in some countries such as France, Spain and Italy. Syndicalism grew out of trade union associations that espoused the utopian vision of one day controlling their industries and, eventually, the political system. The strike became the main weapon of syndicalism. However, it was the **general strike** that made syndicalism revolutionary. The thousands of strikes in Europe during this period presented the potential power of a total work stoppage that would ruin capitalism and dismantle the government. George Sorel's writings about syndicalism in 1908, considered general strike as a mythic belief, the wide spread acceptance of which would prompt collective action by workers.

The movement of the revolting masses must be represented in such a way that the soul of workers may receive a deep and lasting impression capable of evoking as an undivided whole the mass of sentiments which corresponds to the different manifestation of the war undertaken by the people against the ruling class in an unjust technological society. The movement concentrates in the essence of general strike; there is no longer any place for the reconciliation regarding the issues at stake. Everything is clearly mapped out, so that only one interpretation of the new order, namely democracy as a system, is accepted.

The possibility of actual realization of the general strike has been much discussed. To the people who think of themselves as cautious, practical, and scientific, the difficulty of setting general masses of the workers in motion at the same time seems prodigious. Its realization is considered a popular dream and an illusion of youth, soon be discarded. But experience shows that the framing of a future, in some indeterminate time, may, when it is done in a proper way, be very effective. This happens when the anticipations of the future take the form of those myths, which embody all the strongest inclinations of the people which give an aspect of complete reality to the hopes of immediate action by which, more easily than by any other method, people can attain their goal of a just and fair society.

The theory of general strike is proved to be so effective as a motive force that once it has entered the minds of the people, they cannot be controlled by the government or other existing institutional forces. There have been many successful use of general strike in history, with no room here to cite them. One which is recent and best suited in resolving the present demolishing societal situations under capitalistic systems and its replacement by a new system of societal order, is the 1979 revolution in Iran by the full use of the general strike theory.

Operation Ajax was set up by the CIA to overthrow the democratically elected government of the Prime Minister Dr. Mohammad Mossadeg in 1953 and reinstall the Shah, who had fled the country, to the throne of Iran. (See CIA Ajax Operation) Under Mossadeg's leadership the Iranian oil industries were nationalized in 1951, ousting the British Petroleum Company (BP) which had appropriated over 85 percent of profits from the Iranian oil resources since its creation in 1908.

The Prime Minister also advised the monarch to transfer the ruling of the country to people's elected officials and assume a status similar to that of the British monarch. The Shah resisted and under mounting public pressure he was obliged to leave the country. CIA, led by Kermit

Roosevelt, a grandson of Theodor Roosevelt, initiated a coup in Iran to remove Mossadeg. The coup was successful and the royal monarch, Shah Mohammad Reza Pahlavi was brought back to throne which became a virtual dictator. Fearing popular reprisal, his government, supported by the CIA, created SAVAK, a vicious secret police organization, to suppress any decent. However, demonstrations against the Shah's government continued and grew strong by mid 1960s which was brutally put down by the government forces and its most influential leader, Ayatollah Khomeini, was exiled to Iraq and then to France. Opposition demonstrations grew strong again and continued until 1979 during which thousands gave their lives for freedom and tens of thousands were detained and brutally tortured. By 1979 different opposition groups had united behind a common objective of overthrowing and replacing the regime through a general strike. People were facing a government totally supported by the United States, with the strongest and most modern military force in the Middle East, scores of American advisers and the U.S. supported secret police.

First, students poured on the streets nationwide, and oil industry workers stopped work cutting off 80 percent of the government's revenues. Soon work stoppage spread to other sectors of economy, public employees, police, and finally the military, starting disobedience by junior officers and solders under their command. In a matter of few weeks, the whole government fell apart, the Shah was obliged to flee the country, with no major country willing to give him refuge including the United States. A totally new democratic system was established in Iran. Ayatollah Khomeini was brought back as a top religious figure, who a year later took over the power, wrote a new constitution according to which he became the sole power ruling the country. Hard gained democracy and freedom did not last very long. However, the newly established societal system, offering free education, free health care, old age and antipoverty programs, remained intact.

The same opposition process which ousted the monarch in 1953 has been repeating itself, despite sacrifices, and getting stronger each year apparently toward another general strike. The enemies are the same as in 1953, the domestic dictatorial regime and the United States which has caused incredible loss of hundreds of thousand Iranian lives by supporting the monarch's brutal rule before the revolution since 1953 and assisting Saddam Hussein during his invasion of Iran in 1980-1988, as well as imposing economic embargos and pressure on the national economy and people's daily life since 1979. The present unduly strong American objection to Iran's nuclear research authorized under NPT, puzzles informed Iranians since in 1950s, under President Eisenhower, continued until 1979, the U.S. fully cooperated with the Iranian government for the development of the Iranian nuclear energy, "Atom for Peace" program and building about two dozen nuclear energy plants, yet presently, the U.S. is strongly critical of Iran's legally authorized nuclear activities intended for the same purpose, as expressed by the Iranian government, atom for peace. Iranians may accept establishment of a normal diplomatic relations with the United States but never consider U.S. government as a friend because of their painful passed experiences with it since 1953.

ONE:
WHY A NEW
AMERICA IS NEEDED

Only a nation conscious of its present can hope for a bright future. If by employing the knowledge left for us by the past utopians we don't succeed in providing a rational coordination of impulses and thoughts toward restructuring the past utopias, for probably centuries, our civilization will be degenerated into a state of chaotic minor excitements so-called reforms.

Unfortunately, up to the present the technological society has been unable to conceive any vision of the future though many are not satisfied with the welter of minor excitements. A comprehensive, equitable, and satisfying concept of the future is badly and immediately needed. This must be a concept which would provide an overall standard for judging the use of technology for societal equilibrium, with equitable distribution of its fruits among all population. This aim cannot be achieved if technology is used to benefit primarily a small group in its drive for accumulation of wealth and attainment of power. It has already become clear that the material successes of the spirit of capitalism enormously enhanced by the use, or more truly misuse, of technology have not been the outward and visible signs of inward and spiritual grace; it has not caused social justice. It is a visible evidence that technology in the wrong hands can be utterly dangerous to and destructive of human prosperity, happiness, dignity and freedom.

In this regard, it is about time we ask ourselves: why must per capita consumption always increase in order for us to be a healthy society? What do we get for it except the depletion of our finite resources, an enormous amount of junk and garbage, including the atomic and toxic waste which threaten the healthy continuation of our civilization? Are we really happier, healthier or closer to some ideal state of societal life? Why have many of the early societies remained in a relatively balanced relationship with the environment extending for centuries? Why in these societies there was and still is leisure time for conversation, literature, art, music, and enjoyment of the magnificent beauties of the nature? Shouldn't we use technology to provide us with such a pleasurable life rather than employing it for wasteful production and destruction of our environment? Why should we use technology for killing better and more human beings, mass destruction of humans, whole communities and the nature? Shouldn't we use technology for freeing men and women from dull, irksome, distasteful, and uninspiring work, and for enlarging opportunities for more cultivated, enjoyable and creative pursuits?

The facts of our present societal life indicate that material abundance alone does not inevitably lead to spiritual peace of mind, happiness, and pleasure. Among technological societies, ours is the one with the highest rate of crime, accidents, homicides, and mental stress. All these facts of life and circumstances point to the imminent necessity for a practical, satisfying and liberating concept of a futuristic democratic system. The following is a brief presentation of such a concept, labeled properly as **technological democracy,** or **democracy as a system.**

DEMOCRATIC ORGANISM AND ITS COMPONENTS

There are mainly three basic components which together form the organic structure of technological democracy. These are **people, technology,** and **equality of opportunity.** People are the operators of the system; technology is the main tool of operation; equality of opportunity is the scientific basis for the structure of the system and determinant of societal values. The absence of any of them from the daily life's process will be destructive of democracy. **People** consists of **Individuals** who are necessary to operate the system. But these are a **special kind of individuals.** They are well aware and cognizant of the other two components. They know all about the nature of technology and its proper use, and are deeply committed to the idea of equality of opportunity. This required span of knowledge makes them high quality beings that the world has never encountered in masses. Their knowledge is not limited to the normative aspects of the theory but they know how to employ, apply, and operate all these norms in actual process of life. Without these qualifications, no one can fully and meaningfully participate in materializing technological democracy and substantially enjoy its fruits. Fortunately, attaining such knowledge to its minimum necessity, during the stage of transition, is simple and understandable by any person with a high school education.

Technology is the second component of democratic organism. It is mostly a self-operating organ which facilitates and substantially helps the materialization of the contributions from the other two components. Some of the essential contributions of technology to democracy are providing for freedom of information relating to the operation of the socioeconomic and political aspects of life in society; supervising the proper application of the principle of equality of opportunity in government, business, and society as a whole; carrying and supervising the electoral process; providing for free education and certification of the results for each individual; supervising the system of work load for each worker, proper wages and much more. This self controlled electronic system is labeled the Technodem. In a technological society, a true democracy without the Technodem is unthinkable and impossible. For example, because of this system, every worker having complaint about his/her employer can electronically resort to the Technodem. The complain is instantly investigated and reported back to the worker and his employer with needed action to be taken by the latter to remedy the situation, if any. This is the extreme extent of freedom that the Technodem provides and protects. It supervises the application of the principle of equality of opportunity and renders incredible service to the people in all areas of the societal functions It is for this reason that technology constitutes an indispensable component of the democratic organism in modern society. The detailed structure and operation of the Technodem are found in materials referred to at the end of this writing.

The third and most important component of the democratic organism is the **principle of equality of opportunity**. Its application definitely leads toward an equitable society where in national issues such as health care and education, all individuals have equal opportunity of access, and in employment and workplace, each person is entitled to the same opportunity as others with the same level of knowledge and experience. This principle is permanent and universally superior, and at all times, controls the exercise of any human or institutional authority whatsoever. All other principles of society concerned with human rights and liberties are derived from this principle and their boundaries controlled by it. But these boundaries are so broad that any enumeration of human rights will come short of its full extent. Democracy flourishes when one respects equality of opportunity in relations with others and the environment even with future generations.

TWO:

DEMOCRACY AS
A SYSTEM

Despite some two centuries of efforts to establish a more just society through democratic means, today there is no single nation in the world where democracy has been established in its true sense including Sweden and Switzerland known as the two most democratic countries in the Western world.

During the last two centuries, political democracy has been the center of attraction by practitioners for the main purpose of establishing a legitimate system to maintain individual and property rights and protect the operation of capitalism. It was not until after the Second World War that capitalism became monopolistic in a way that drew serious attention. It was during the last five decades that monopoly capitalism, which had its roots in the late nineteenth and early twentieth centuries, established its firm grip on the American economy as well as government and, through the power and influence of the latter, on the economy and resources of many developing countries. Similar developments, though in a less dramatic manner, were followed by other industrialized countries. It has also been during these decades that different scholars have paid increasing attention to the erosion of individual rights, liberties, extension of poverty and accelerating class stratification under the technological monopolistic capitalism. Technology which has been mainly controlled by the economic elite, has played a significant role in this process of degradation and subjugation.

In technological democracy, the term democracy is looked upon not just from political viewpoint but as a system embracing all political, economic and social components of society. Simply, the term democracy, in its true and full meaning, means political, economic, and social democracies all put together as a system. If any of these component parts is missing, democracy is defective to that extent and a true democracy does not exist.

In the United States, for example, there is no economic democracy, and social democracy is substantially missing. This makes the existing political democracy subject to prevailing undemocratic economic and social norms, and thus, highly defective and in some respects meaningless. The lack of economic democracy is evident by the control of economy by a small economic elite, by exploitation of workers and consumers, and by economic class stratification. The lack of social democracy I visualized through the practice of racism, sexism, lack of appropriate and equal educational opportunities, lack of national health care, lack of opportunities in housing, transportation, adequate and proper old age benefits. The lack of political democracy is evidenced by corrupt electoral process, manipulated voter registration system, selection of candidates by the economic elite and spending enormous amount of money for their election. The outcome is a corrupt pro-elite and pro-war government; since wars are highly profitable for the corporate elite; billions of dollars of taxpayers money is spent in arms, equipments and military training for mass destruction and killing; invade a selected country with important natural resources; commit mass destruction and killing; then receiving billions of taxpayers money in contracts to reconstruct it. Wars are extremely profitable business for the corporate elite and incredible loss for taxpayers of resources that could be used for domestic development and providing millions of employment opportunities.

Technological democracy is thus a societal system by itself quite distinguished from the existing systems of capitalism or socialism. It extends to all aspects of a societal life. Its understanding is quite simple since its operation and value system depends mainly on the application of a single principle of equality of opportunity to all aspects of life. It is the proper structure and operation of the society under this principle which is substantially different from those existing at the present; and it is this part that requires a new set of knowledge and understanding.

EQUALITY OF OPPORTUNITY

In a simple definition, the term of equality of opportunity means that every individual in technological democratic society enjoys equal opportunity of access to political, economic, and social means. However, its proper application is somehow complex and requires particular attention to its meaning in its application to certain situations. Presentation of economic democracy which follows will clarify most of these situations.

ECONOMIC DEMOCRACY

The manner by which property is produced, owned, and used, determines the economic structure of society and, to a substantial degree, its social and political characteristics. A necessary condition for economic democracy is the equitable distribution of capital among the people and dispersed control over its use.

The principle of equality of opportunity prescribes that no one in technological democracy should be allowed to gain opportunity over others through accumulation of wealth by profits or free transfer. This principle is known as **prohibition of unjust enrichment.** Such accumulation is allowed only through individual's own labor. Thus, no one can be enriched through inheritance or receiving property or assets without a comparable compensation. The reason is that such enrichment will disturb equality of opportunity by increasing one's opportunity, without his personal efforts, over those of others. Inheritance is allowed only to the extent that it does not affect equality of opportunity, level of which will be calculated annually by the Technodem and approved by the National Economic Council. As the general distribution of wealth moves toward becoming more and more equitable, the level of inheritance is adjusted accordingly. The same will apply to the maximum value of gifts people like to give one another in special occasions which does not cause any change in equality of opportunity between the receiver and others. Simply, no such gift should amount to unjust enrichment.

Inheritance and bequest of large amount of wealth have been the main factors which have kept wealthy families in control of the means of production and distribution for generations. Therefore, the concept of **prohibition of unjust enrichment** has been the outcome of application of the principle of equality of opportunity. Appropriation of social surplus or profit is another form of unjust enrichment since the capitalist receives it through the exploitation of workers as well as consumers. Such appropriation unjustly enhances the opportunity of the capitalist against workers and others.

Consequently, by the prohibition of unjust enrichment in a capitalist society like the United States, the already accumulated wealth of the economic elite tends to disintegrate gradually and disappear by two manners. First, by the prohibition of inheritance and other unjust enrichments, such as trusts and free bequests; and second, by the prohibition of profits, an invisible kind of unjust enrichment, which has been the main source of accumulation of wealth. The outcome is the equitable distribution of wealth among the working class. Along with these changes, as the time goes by, the society and the production system tend to become more dynamic because of increasing incentives induced by the workers who are now becoming the owners of capital.

CAPITAL AND CAPITAL ACCUMULATION

While capital is still one of the main forces of production, its characteristics is quite different with that under capitalism or socialism. Accumulation of capital is a direct result of savings by the labor force rather than the consequence of any exploitation. Returns from its use also is not through exploitation. Though no profits are allowed the capital invested for production is subject to a return, rate of which is determined periodically by the National Economic Council, a national agency with no line function. The ownership of assets from non-transferable shares of production firms (explained later) owned by each worker and a part from his or her other assets revert to the Public Consumption Fund after his or her death according to the principle of **prohibition of unjust enrichment** in order to maintain equality of opportunity.

Apart from the capital accumulated through savings from a worker's pay, each worker also has another source of capital accumulation which is a determined number of shares of his employer's firm he receives every month along with his salary, weekly or by-weekly pay. This process gradually transfers capital from the capitalist to the worker allowing him or her a voice in the operation of the firm. As a result, ultimately the workers together owning the majority of shares of the company take over the operation of the firm terminating the traditional dominance and control by the capitalist elite. A unique and fantastic result is attained by this process of transition; the distinction between the capitalist and working class disappears and both join together into one. The workers are those who also own the capital. Capitalism disappears from the society with all its evil characteristics.

The accumulated capital by the workers through the ownership of production firms have several beneficial social consequences. Since it is non-transferable, it remain under the ownership of the worker providing him with income sufficient for a modest but comfortable living standards after retirement. It replaces the present Social Security system but owned and managed personally by each worker. For this program, the worker does not pay any tax as it is paid for Social Security; the money comes from the worker's employer in the form of shares of the firm; it is not controlled by the government but individually by the worker; unlike Social Security program, the worker receives income from the capital he or she accumulate each year; since these assets are, like the Social Security, for old age benefits, they cannot be transferred to anyone else. Since, at the present any person receiving Social Security benefit does not receive anything after his or her death here, here also, after the worker's death the non-transferable assets reverts to the Public Consumption Fund providing for free health care, education, and other beneficial services for all. At the same time, these shares are sold in the open market, by this agency, purchased by different production firms to be transferred gradually, as a part from their pay, to the incoming new generation of workers. In reality this is a social capital in circulation providing a variety of beneficial functions, all under private and individual control.

WORKING CLASS UNDER TECHNOLOGICAL DEMOCRACY

Technological democracy eliminates distinction between the capitalist and the working class and gradually molds them into one. It must be noted that the term working class under this theory refers to anyone working for a production firm including managers, administrators, and professionals. This new mode of production is attained by the application of the principle of equality of opportunity. It becomes more clarified when the concept of position classification and employment is discussed below. It eliminates exploitation and makes the worker a full participant in production and distribution process. Equality of opportunity is not an abstract principle. It is subject to relativity based on reason, logic and reasonableness. In the production process, it creates different opportunity levels based on individual's intelligence, education and experience.

Opportunity levels are of two kinds: initial and gained. The former is based on each individual's natural competence without counting the effect of outside factors such as education and experience. From this viewpoint, individuals are not born with equal opportunities mentally, physically or otherwise. The gained level of opportunity is attained through the effect of outside factors such as education and experience. In technological democratic society, education and experience opportunities are equally available to all. Therefore, though individuals start life with unequal opportunities, they can move up their level of opportunity toward equalizing it with those of higher initial opportunity. However, each individual has a ceiling in his level of opportunity based on the quality of his initial opportunity level and intelligence. This ceiling can be attained only by the maximum use of one's capabilities. The crucial point in technological democracy is that everyone within each opportunity level has the same opportunity as the others within the same level. This will become more clear when the subject of employment is discussed later.

Equality of opportunity will tend also equalize what is called **lost opportunity**. This occurs when a person is deprived or denied the opportunity to raise the level of his competence or when, despite having competence, is not granted equal opportunity in employment. Both of these are the characteristics of a capitalistic system and very unlikely to happen in a technological democratic society. It is possible to occur during the transition period and disappear when the system approaches the stage of full democracy.

SHARED OPPORTUNITY AND EMPLOYMENT RIGHTS

Equality of opportunity guarantees every individual the right for employment. There is no equality of opportunity present between those who are employed and those who are unemployed but with the same competence. Equality of opportunity requires that each institution must provide unemployed individual with an appropriate employment opportunity corresponding to his or her level of competency.

This is made possible by the application of the principle of **shared opportunity** which is derived from the principle of equality of opportunity. It applies to the situation where there are unemployed individuals without appropriate employment opportunity. To equalize their opportunity with those of employed workers within the same level of competence, each working individual gives up a small portion of his employment opportunity to provide equal employment opportunity for those seeking employment. For example, if nationwide 100 million workers give up one hour work of their 40-hour-per-week. It will create 100 million hours of employment opportunity or 2.5 million full time new positions. This is a simplified example, in actual situation it applies, in each production firm, to a specific line of production and in a specific area of competence comparable to those seeking employment. The concept of supply and demand at each level of employment stabilizes the employment market for this level. Shared opportunity is a very important concept; it allows the principle of equality of opportunity to prevail causing full employment and lifetime job security for anyone desiring to work.

THE WAGE SYSTEM

At every level of employment hierarchy, compensation is based on the level of required competence and experience. The general level of compensation is determined by a general position classification at the national level calculated and established by the National Economic Council by the assistance of the Technodem. The Technodem, by having access to prices of all goods and services, calculates and reports to the Council the amount of minimum wage required for a minimum living standard, and the Council establishes the classification of the wage system accordingly. This classification model is fed to the Technodem equipped to supervise its application in every institution hiring workers. Each production firm then establishes its own position classification according to this national model including detailed level of required qualification for each position and corresponding compensation level within the range prescribed by the national model.

Since all production systems are computerized and they are required to connect all their operation to the Technodem, this kind of position classification nationwide becomes a simple process and nearly uniform everywhere. As soon as the position classification is completed in any firm or those in existence are revised each is checked against the national standards by the Technodem in a matter of seconds and deviation in any firm, if any, is pointed out to that firm for consideration and correction.

The national position classification model has several substantial benefits:

1. It harmonizes and standardizes all available positions, private as well as public.

2. It equalizes the pay system, with similar pay for similar position.

3. It eliminates the union bargaining and thus eliminates unionization for economic purposes.

4. It simplifies position and pay classification at the institutional level, since there is a periodically updated national model to follow.

5. It democratizes the work system by providing equality of opportunity in similar positions with similar pay.

6. It allows regional agencies to supervise the proper and uniform application of the national standards.

7. It bestows discretion on each institution to go about establishing its own job and pay classification in accordance within framework of the national model.

8. It gives every worker an opportunity to evaluate his or her position, comparing it with the national standard, and in the case of discrepancy check the issue with the Technodem, which instantly responds to it and informs the worker if there is any discrepancy, and at the same time, informs his or her employer to correct it. If the discrepancy is not corrected, both the Technodem and the worker inform the regional classification office, The employer has no other recourse but to correct the discrepancy. In this way, position classification in each institution is scrutinized by its workers and brought to the level prescribed by the national standards while protecting workers rights and freedom.

Compensation for each position consists of two parts. First, a cash payment, the wage, sufficient to provide a worker, at least, with a modest but convenient living standard. Second, payment in stocks of the employee's firm to the extent that the return from their accumulation in thirty years of employment would be sufficient in providing for a comfortable living standard after retirement. The amount of stocks received by each worker corresponds to certain percentage of the wage received determined by the National Economic Council. Thus, as the wage increases, so does the amount of corresponding stocks.

Stock allocations take place each month. Gradually, it transfers capital from the capitalist to the working class. At the end of transition, despite the total private ownership of the means of production, there is no separation between capital and labor. The capitalist elite disappears, and through the ownership of capital, the working class governs the policy-making and management processes through their managers and administrators.

As mentioned above, these stocks are not transferable since they are substitute to the present Social Security system by being the source of income during the retirement years. They transfer the ownership of capital from the capitalist to the workers; unlike the present Social Security system, they provide additional and increasing income to the worker during his or her working years which can be used according to desire of the receiver; they provide the worker with an independent and adequate retirement and old age benefits; and ultimately, they revert to the public domain after the death of the beneficiary, to be used to support the pay system for the upcoming generation. However, for the purpose of diversification, these stocks can be exchanged in the stock market with non-transferable stocks of other firms.

EDUCATION AND THE WORK SYSTEM

In a technological democracy, after twelve years of general education, the work system and education merge together. Every individual is required to complete the general education program. It consists of four years of preschool education starting at age three up to seven; four years of elementary and four years of secondary education. It consists of a condensed curricula from grade one through twelve. It is the most important part of each individual's education and enormously effective in the future competence of the work force. The equality of opportunity requires that this education be available to all free of any charge or obstacle.

After completing this required program of education, the person who is about fifteen years old, starts to work part-time while continuing his education full-time. In a technological democratic society, a worker's life has two distinguished aspects. One is his development as a conscious human being, necessary for true participation in a democratic society. As a **democratic person**, he is deeply devoted to the principle of democracy, equality of opportunity in particular and its application in every aspect of the societal life. To attain this level of competence, the individual receives a broad education in the area of humanities including languages, literature, history, philosophy, art and music; non-professional aspects of social sciences including political science, economics, sociology, psychology, and geography; natural sciences including biology, physics, chemistry, geology, botany and environmental science; and of course mathematics which is an absolute necessity to better and simpler understanding of all above stated areas of knowledge and daily life.

It may be properly questioned the reason for acquiring knowledge in all these fields mentioned above. To become a democratic person, one needs a deep understanding of the purpose of life and being; truth, honesty, humility and integrity in association and interaction with others; respect to the nature, environment and other beings; and unselfishness in social, economic and political spheres of life. Moreover, as a democratic person one has to understand, through education, practice, and experience, the complex meaning and application of the principle of equality of opportunity. It is only through appropriate understanding and application of this principle that socioeconomic and political framework of each individual's personality is determined, expansion of one's freedoms and their limitations are distinguished.

The core part of this liberal and humanistic education is achieved through the twelve years of required general education, age three to fifteen. However, to remain update in rapidly changing technological and social conditions, the education is continued beyond this level and through all working years of each individual. As part of this continued education, along with technical and professional subjects, each worker is required to take each year a certain prescribed number of courses in the general education area, toward enhancing his general and cultural knowledge including of democracy as a system and as applied in daily life.

The other aspect of the worker's life relates to his work, his area of specialty, his proficiency, and productiveness. Each individual when he or she starts to work at the age of fifteen, devotes half of his educational program to professional or technical subjects, and the other half to liberal arts education, and continues the same way for all of his working years. The first seven years he works part-time and studies full time. He takes about 12 credit hours per semester under the present system or a total of

168 credits in seven years, equivalent of an MA degree. At the age 22 and thereafter, he or she works full time and continues his or her education part-time, about 6 credits per semester as a part from his work hours, equally divided between technical-professional and liberal arts areas. In fact education becomes part of the worker's work program. For example, on a 40-hour per week work schedule, he works for 32 hours and studies for 8 hours. All presently extensive in-service training programs are discarded.

There is also another aspect to worker's education. It is through experience. On the one hand, in his workplace, experience teaches him the ways he can turn his or her knowledge into efficient and productive action. On the other, how to use his liberal art education for better serving his fellow citizens and his community even the nation and how to enjoy his leisure time fruitfully and benefit from interactions with others.

HOW TO START THE TRANSITION

The essential demand must be an amendment to the U.S. Constitution establishing equality of opportunity as a fundamental right of every American in every aspect of daily life. The U.S. Constitution literally recognizes this right but it needs a formal recognition, specification and clarification. The big obstacle would be its effect on the economic elite particularly relating to inheritance and free transfer of wealth. To overcome this, Congress may be allowed to establish the initial limit on inheritance at, for example, five million dollars. Since only 4 percent of Americans have assets above this limit, ratification of the amendment in three-forth of the states will be easy. The main obstacle may be the U.S. Senate which may require public pressure forcing it to go along. If this became impossible, then the demand should be directed to the establishment of a National Constitutional Convention to devise a new constitution for a technological democratic society as it was done some 200 years ago in establishing a new system of society and government. If the amendment was proposed and ratified, there will be no need for Constitutional Convention because the gradual application of equality of opportunity will gradually transform the present system to technological democracy under the concept of democracy as a system similar to what is presented in this writing. The wealth will be equitably distributed among the people; the work and pay system will be harmonized and uniform among all production institutions; healthcare, education, and old-age benefits will be guaranteed for all people.

THREE:
THE GOVERNMENT UNDER TECHNOLOGICAL DEMOCRACY

The government that governs the least is the best. This is the motto behind the structure and function of government in technological democracy. Compared to the present system, the size of the national government is reduced, at the most, to about 40 percent of its present size; and the state government, to 60 percent. But there is some 10 percent increase in the size of the local government. The main objective in a technological democracy is to allow opportunities for individual freedom and dignity in a way that no one is exploited economically, socially or politically. First, control over the means of production and distribution of goods and services is gradually taken away from the capitalist group and government and returned to the working class through the application of the principle of equality of opportunity. There are no profits made and thus exploitation of both workers and consumers is eliminated. The workers, consisting of the members of the board of

43

directors, top executives, managers, all the way down to the lowest level of employment, become the owners and take over the operation of every firm. Second, nearly 90 percent of the domestic line functions of the national government and about 60 percent of the state line functions are eliminated and to that extent individuals are liberated from public control or regulation. Furthermore, the government is also obliged to abide by the principle of equality of opportunity. Among other things it means that all its functions and policies must be open to the public by feeding them into the Technodem. It cannot keep anything secret or confidential. Every individual has equal opportunity of access to government archives. There are no such thing as classified information except those dealing with narrowly defined national security matters. Thus, the national government is an open and comparatively small bureaucracy. Defense establishment is also highly curtailed in size; because, in technological democracy the essence of strength is not in military might and weapons, of mass destruction but in the strength of its citizens mind and commitment. As technological democracy advances in other countries, there will be no need for military forces. Elimination of military element will mark the elimination of modern barbarism and the disappearance of the greatest evil haunting humanity and its well being for thousands of years.

If the government has no line functions, there is no need for the kind of vast, wasteful, and expensive bureaucracy which presently characterizes the government under capitalism as well as socialism. The vast amount of money used for its maintenance is channeled for productive purposes. Citizens are also relieved from its dominance and intrusion in their daily affairs. The government at every level, while having extremely important functions is highly simplified, much closer to, and within easy reach of the people. It is further reduced in size as the society moves toward full democracy. Most of the public functions are transferred to production firms, social organizations, and local institutions. The detailed presentation of the structure and functions of government at different levels of national, state and local is not possible in this short essay. The following nine figures show how unique and totally different the new system is; these figures also visually demonstrate

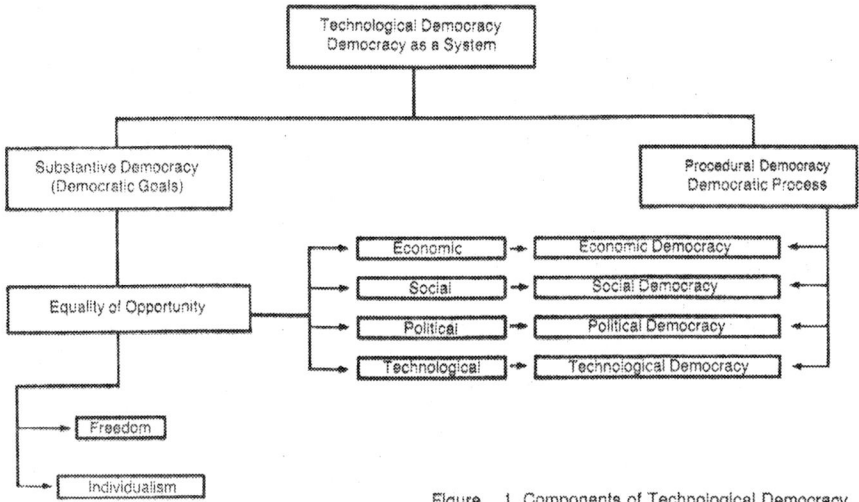

Figure 1. Components of Technological Democracy

Figure 2. Prerequisites of Political Equality of Opportunity

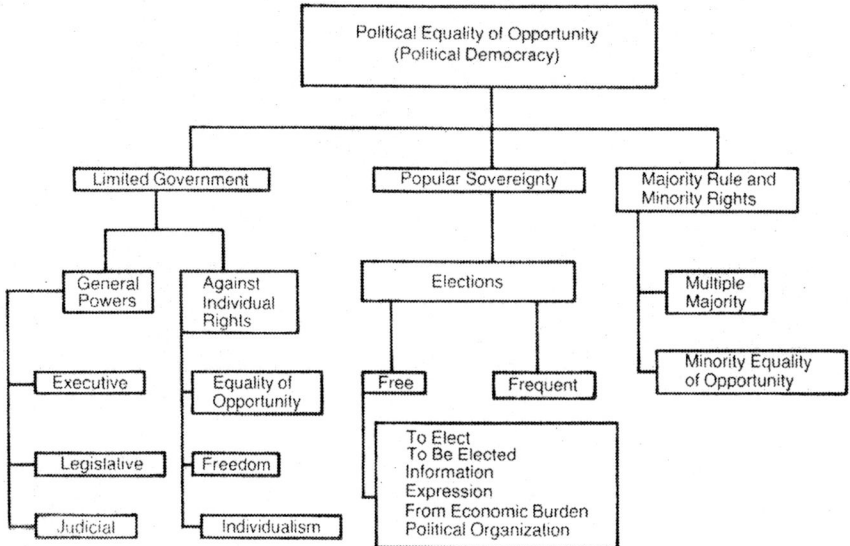

its structure and functions in brief. To know more and in detail how this new society and its public institutions work, reference to the author's major publications is needed which are cited at the end of this writing.

Figure 1 points out the two major components of democracy, substantive and procedural, both of which must be present for democracy to materialize. It also presents the general structure of democracy as a system embodying all economic, social, and political aspects of life.

Figure 2 demonstrates the way political democracy is materialized by the application of the principle of equality of opportunity, by which, the government cannot impose any restriction on individual rights and freedoms; under which, electoral process is free from any interference. People are free to elect and be elected; there are freedom of information and expression in electoral as well as legislative process; elections are free from any economic or financial burden, meaning that no money is to be collected or spent by anyone for electoral purpose; and every individual or group has the same opportunity as the others in electoral and legislative matters.

Figure 3 shows the effect of equality of opportunity in the operation of economy, including the new nature of the capital, its ownership and use; workers, their rights as workers and owners of capital; Sharp restrictions on government interference in the operation of economy.

Figure 4 demonstrates the extreme importance of the Technodem as the guardian of the principle of equality of opportunity, and the vast areas in societal life that it supervises and extends a helping hand when needed or asked for. The Figure also shows the role of technology in the process of production of goods and services.

Figure 5 presents the structure and function of the National Legislative and Coordination Assembly, which is the most important and powerful body of the national government. It supervises and approves

Figure 3. Prerequisites of Economic Equality of Opportunity

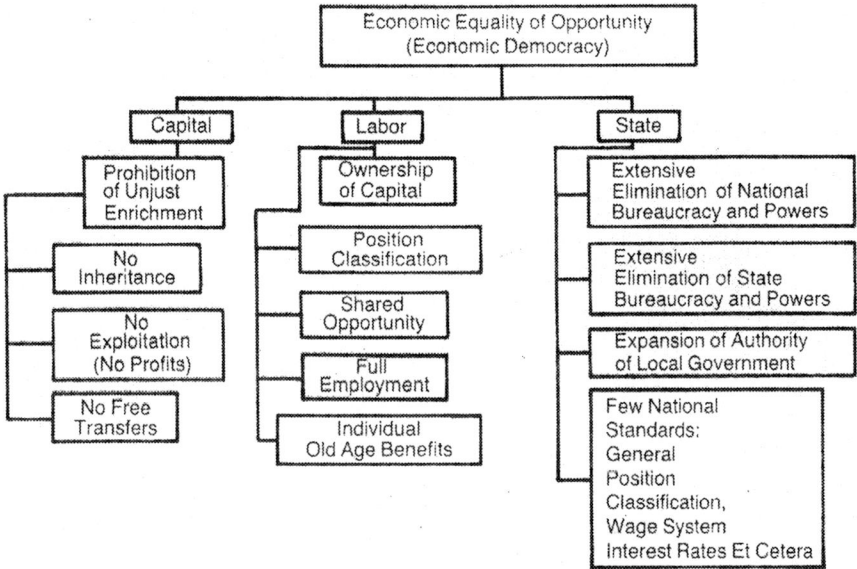

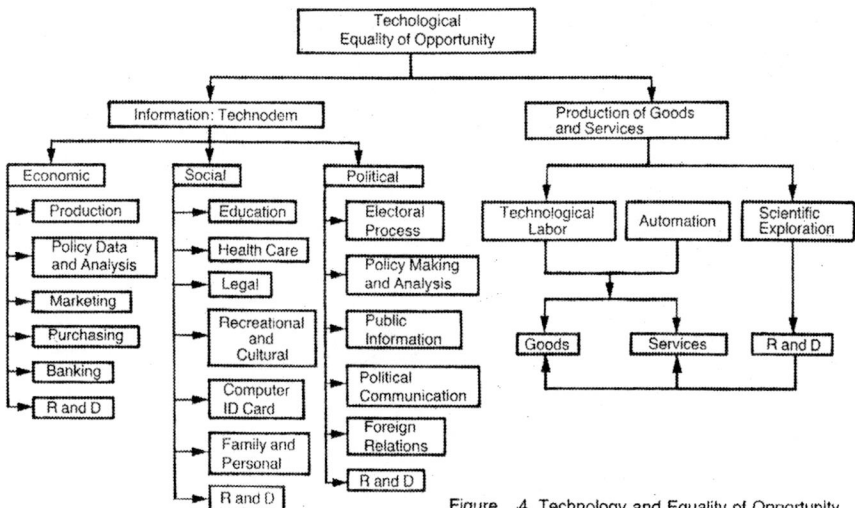

Figure 4. Technology and Equality of Opportunity

the standards established by four powerful councils. It is important to notice that none of these councils or the assembly has line functions. They establish the standards and regulations that must be followed or executed by the private sector, local and state governments.

The Economic and Production Council establishes the national position and pay classification model to be followed by all production institutions, supervised by the Technodem. The Council determines the rules about the ownership and use of capital and its maximum annual rate of return, for example: 5 percent. It is possible for the Council not to establish any specific rate of return and leave it for the market to determine it for each institution, because the capital is owned by the workers and return from it goes to all of them in proportion of shares each owns. The Council also establishes regulations concerning the extraction or use of the national resources.

The Health and Education Council establishes the model system for the 12-year general education, its required curricula, and its operation. It also determines the general structure and operation of the national healthcare system to be carried out by the local and state governments.

The International Affairs Council deals with the framework of activities of the national executive branch, rules and regulations to be followed in dealing with other countries and international organizations in all necessary areas.

The Judicial Council drafts laws necessary for the operation of the national judiciary, rules and regulations regarding the judicial procedure, criminal and civil laws applied at the national level.

Figure 6 presents the application of equality of opportunity to social issues particularly in the areas of education and healthcare, already discussed above.

Figure 7 Shows the basic structure of the executive and judicial branches of the national government with some 80 percent decrease in

Figure , ·5. The Basic Structure of National Government, Legislative and Policy Branch

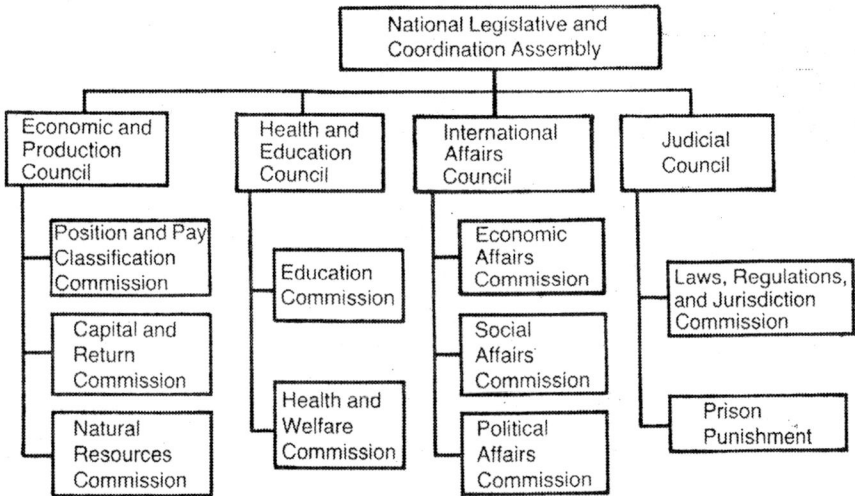

Figure ·6. Prerequisites of Social Equality of Opportunity

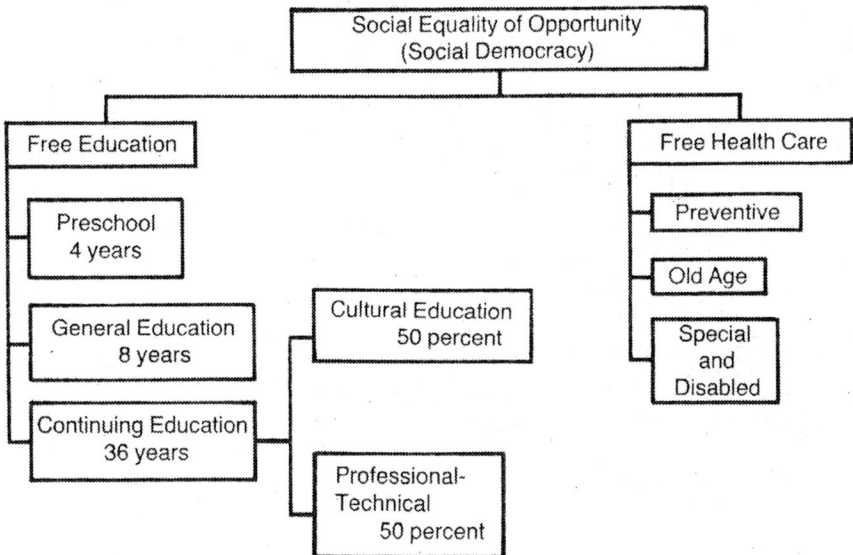

their size and with highly simplified bureaucracy in the rest. Each branch is administered by a council making it more responsive to public opinion. Presidential Council is composed of seven members, with one seven-year term, one council member being elected each year. The senior member, with six years of experience in the council, becomes president of the country for one year. Decisions, which are mostly of international nature, are made by the majority vote of the members and the President is obliged to execute them even he had voted with the minority.

Figure 8 illustrates the structure and functions of the state government. The Governor functions in cooperation with the State Legislative and Coordinating Assembly. As the Figure shows the state functions and bureaucracy are highly diminished and simplified.

Figure 9 presents the structure and functions of the local government, simplified in some areas and extended in others. It has close supervision of production firms, educational system, healthcare, taxes and revenues, and actual responsibility in administrating all social, financial, and customary municipal functions. It is important to notice that no government, organization or groups, except for those intending to run for any elective office is involved in electoral process. This eliminates a huge bureaucracy, registration process, corruption, fraud, fundraising, etc. The Technodem is responsible to carry out all electoral process, and no human hands except those of the candidates in the beginning and the voters at the end are involved in the whole electoral process.

Figure 7. The Basic Structure of National Government

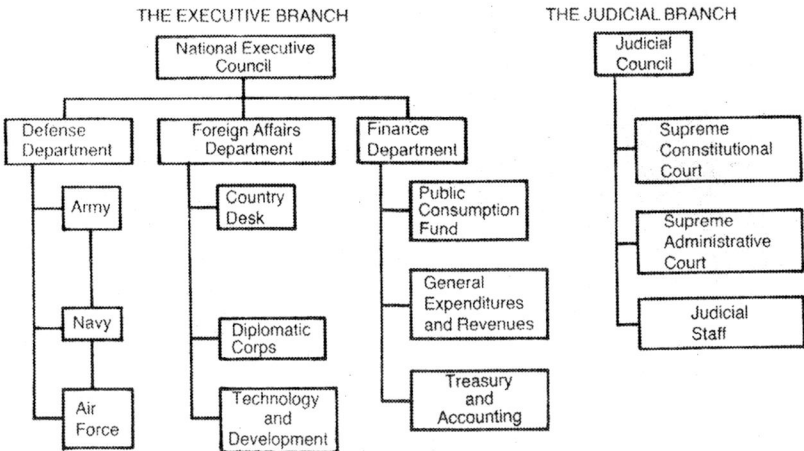

THE EXECUTIVE BRANCH

National Executive Council

- Defense Department
  - Army
  - Navy
  - Air Force
- Foreign Affairs Department
  - Country Desk
  - Diplomatic Corps
  - Technology and Development
- Finance Department
  - Public Consumption Fund
  - General Expenditures and Revenues
  - Treasury and Accounting

THE JUDICIAL BRANCH

Judicial Council

- Supreme Connstitutional Court
- Supreme Administrative Court
- Judicial Staff

The Basic Structure

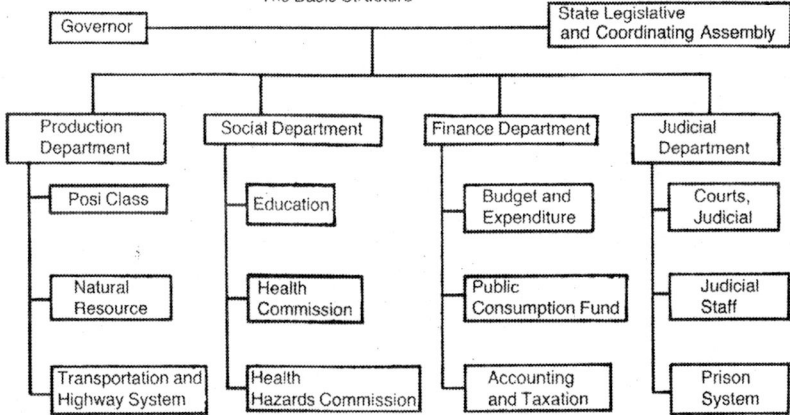

Governor — State Legislative and Coordinating Assembly

- Production Department
  - Posi Class
  - Natural Resource
  - Transportation and Highway System
- Social Department
  - Education
  - Health Commission
  - Health Hazards Commission
- Finance Department
  - Budget and Expenditure
  - Public Consumption Fund
  - Accounting and Taxation
- Judicial Department
  - Courts, Judicial
  - Judicial Staff
  - Prison System

Figure 9. The Basic Structure of Local Government

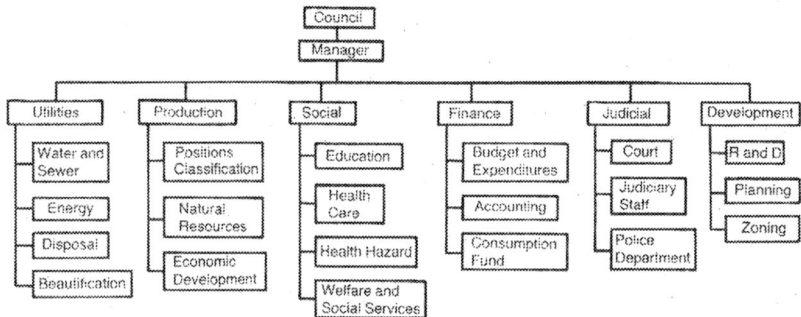

Council

Manager

- Utilities
  - Water and Sewer
  - Energy
  - Disposal
  - Beautification
- Production
  - Positions Classification
  - Natural Resources
  - Economic Development
- Social
  - Education
  - Health Care
  - Health Hazard
  - Welfare and Social Services
- Finance
  - Budget and Expenditures
  - Accounting
  - Consumption Fund
- Judicial
  - Court
  - Judiciary Staff
  - Police Department
- Development
  - R and D
  - Planning
  - Zoning

FOUR:
SOME CHARACTERISTICS OF TECHNOLOGICAL DEMOCRACY

In moving toward technological democracy, the task is not just to substantially reform the traditional ideas and structures of "democratic capitalism" or "democratic socialism," but to establish a totally new system. A system that will give life and concrete content to a technological society through norms and institutions that are democratic, pragmatic as well as practical in a highly industrialized and densely populated society and rapidly changing social and technological environment. The economic and technological means of extraordinary dimensions must be directed by the people, each according to his or her capability, to the benefit of each and all while causing the government to be reduced to its minimum size.

In a technological democracy, the social goal and common purpose, for which society is to be organized, concern itself in providing equality of opportunity for everyone. In such an accomplished society:

1. Everyone starts life from the scratch. There are neither rich nor poor under the present meaning of the terms.

2. Everyone receives 12 years of free general education up to the age 15.

3. Everyone starts to work part-time at age 15, and starts full-time at the age 22.

4. Everyone continues his/her education full-time after the age of 15, while working part-time, and continues part-time after the age of 22, as a part from his/her work program, until retirement. Such education consists of a balanced combination of technical-professional, liberal arts, and humanities subjects. It is reduced to two courses on each subject per year after the age 22, when the worker assumes full-time position.

5. Everyone receives free health and preventive care for life.

6. Everyone, starting from zero, gradually becomes a part owner of production of goods and services. These ownership shares, which replaces the present Social Security system but fully privatized, are destined for the support of the owner after his/her retirement, and thus are not transferable.

7. Everyone works full-time for at least 30 years or equivalent of it.

8. Equivalent to one-fifth of the working hours are allocated to education. Accordingly, for a 40 hours per week work, the person works for 32 hours and studies for 8 hours.

9. Promotion is based on the level of education and years of experience, liberal art education having the same importance as the technical or professional.

10. The age of retirement depends on the supply of the young labor force for the purpose of allowing them equal opportunity for employment. However, to guarantee a comfortable retirement life, no

capable person works for less than 25 years full-time before retirement. The general retirement occurs after 30 years of full-time work.

11. After retirement, which more likely occurs when an individual is in his early 50s, he or she has enough non-transferable assets accumulated to bring him or her returns sufficient for a comfortable living standards. In addition, through his or her personal savings, he or she has other transferable assets under his or her full control.

12. All elective public positions:

a. Require very high qualifications relating to education and experience.

b. Are temporary and no one is elected for the same office for more than one term. Besides other benefits, this also allows opportunities to a greater number of well qualified retired citizens to hold public office and serve the people.

c. These two requirements would allow a better chance of being elected to retired individuals since they are better educated and well experienced and are not looking for a permanent position. They are still young, but matured and capable of fruitful participation in the public policy-making process and public service.

13. As a result of democratic norms and technological developments, family life is transformed from its traditional form into a democratic unit; parents being responsible, though in a different manner, for upbringing of the children up to the age of 15, after which the child, who is considered an adult, enters the labor market and is considered independent.

14 By the time of retirement, the family, more likely because of voluntary birth and population control, has no children to take care of; and free from this responsibility, the couple, if they desire to remain together, has very fruitful, still productive, dynamic, and enjoyable life.

15. After death, a substantial part of an individual's wealth, according to the principle of equality of opportunity, is returned to society, through the Public Consumption Fund, to sustain free services such as health care and education for the new generation which is also to start from the scratch.

16. Though some individuals accumulate more wealth than others, the difference is not so great to cause class distinction. Furthermore, such difference is only for the life of the person and disappears upon his death. In reality, this is a classless society with minor variations in material ownership.

17. An individual's obligatory relationship is within his family and his workplace. Outside these areas, he remains free to enjoy life with a great many things and means accessible to him in an infinite variety of combinations.

18. In its narrow application, equality of opportunity does not allow individual competition where the intention is to take opportunity from someone against whom the individual is competing. However, equality of opportunity not only allows but encourages each individual to compete against himself or herself to become better than what he or she already is. This is quite different from competing against a designated person even it may give the same result. Open competition is the backbone of the democratic market operation, but, it is free of fraudulence, propaganda, and false commercials. Self competition should be the motto of production here as well. It causes the production of better goods or services resulting in marketing success The exact specifications of the products are stated and left to the consumer to make the choice. Unlike the present situation where commercials are forced on the people by being inserted into television or radio programs, no one is forced, through any means, to watch or listen to commercials.

19. The wealth of a society is the sum total of individual wealth plus all natural and other resources which belong to the society as a whole.

However, the important part of the wealth of a society is not economic and material, but technological in the form of knowledge, experience, and means which is the way of doing things.

20. More important than the production of wealth is its equitable distribution among the working class, subject only to the level of knowledge, and experience. Every worker receives nearly the same amount of income in the full period of his or her work as the others. Each worker starts with the minimum wage and gets more as he or she climbs the ladder to higher positions. By the time of retirement, each worker is a high ranking official in his or her firm.

21. In a democratic system, there is no class structure or class distinction. Differentiation is only at the work place, based on the level of knowledge, experience, and expertise. Working class refers to all working individuals including members of the board of directors, chief executives down to the least experienced.

22. The proper function of government is to establish, maintain and periodically revise the standards required by the principle of equality of opportunity, particularly relating to division of labor and compensation. The national government has no domestic line functions except some supervisory authority in the areas relating to the national consumption fund such as education, healthcare, and corresponding standards. Government is reduced to its minimum functional size.

23. Private wealth totally belongs to the individual for life. It is a wealth initiated, created, and accumulated through his/her own labor, use of his/her assets and not through profits by exploiting others.

24. Public wealth mainly constitutes of the society's natural resources. They belong to the society as a whole, and therefore, net proceeds created belong to the people. Equality of opportunity does not allow any private ownership of natural resources such as oil, gas, minerals, and forests. Such resources may be leased to specific firms to operate. Whatever is left after

paying for all expenses including depreciation of tool, machineries and other properties used for production purpose, goes to Public Consumption Fund and used for public benefit.

25. The electoral system is managed by the Technodem, The only thing a candidate needs to do is to enter his or her name for the office he or she seeks to be elected, into the Technodem's list for that office. No additional information is needed, because the Technodem knows all about each individual in the society. It will present each individual's qualifications in three categories: personal, educational, and experience, and rank each candidate in each category. However, each candidate may have his or her own electoral website and may place in it additional information he may think beneficial for his campaign. No voter is obliged to vote for Technodem's first choice, Each voter selects his or her candidate from this list and votes for him or her through the Technodem on the election day.

26. Political parties as we know of them today are eliminated since there is no need or justification for their existance or other organizations for electoral purpose. The electoral process is electronic, simple, and abuse free; during the election day, each qualified individual inserts his or her electronic ID card into the computer, it is checked against his or her background. If qualified he or she votes from anyplace in the world for the candidate of his or her choice for the national, state or local office.

27. There is a total private ownership of the means of production of goods and services.

28. Giant corporations are automatically disintegrated into several smaller institutions once the workers take over the management. Huge overhead expenditures are saved.

29. A new free market economy is established with fair and open competition based on equality of opportunity.

30. No individual taxes, no property taxes, and no social security taxes.

31. There is protection of environment, preservation of natural resources, and meaningful use of them for public benefit and keeping them in proper shape for the future generations

MORALITY UNDER TECHNOLOGICAL DEMOCRACY

The moral boundaries of technological democracy are very broad based on the principle of equality of opportunity. No conceivable common ethical code can be comprehensive enough to cover nearly boundless domain of these moral possibilities relating to such values as honesty, integrity, humility and freedom. It is impossible for any mind to comprehend the infinite variety of individual freedoms and good deeds ensuing from this foundation of morality. Whether one's interests center around his or her own well-being, or the welfare of others, regardless how broad and expanded these interests may be, the end that the individual may be concerned with, is always only an infinitesimal fraction of what could be possible under this democratic system. It is within these nearly limitless confines that the individual strives for his life liberty and pursuit of happiness.

We cannot judge or evaluate the characteristics of technological democracy by employing our present values and means of measurement or justification. We must rise and place ourselves on the proper plateau of knowledge and understanding before we start making evaluation and judgment about the moral and ethical values inherent in a technological democratic society. As technology advances, the need for ideological and futuristic concepts increases in exponential scale, because technology has greatly widened the span of options and, at the same time, it has made the choice a necessity.

The progress of a society and its members are not separate from one another. The development of society results from the expression, by the people, of deep seated forces of democratic norms which come to materialize only by an infinitely slow and cumbersome process of mutual adjustments. A basic force in democratization is the understanding that progress is not a matter of mechanical contrivance, but depends on the enrichment of mind and spirit in democratic principles and materializing them through meaningful and vigorous action. For the United States, operating under a strong capitalist system, it has to be through awakening a national consciousness about the evils of capitalism and the nature of a futuristic technological democracy. This would tend to create a committed, strong, and unified movement to materialize such democratic society. This essay offers the interested and active individuals in the search and materializing a just and fair society, the goal they are seeking and how to go about to materialize it. But, in the United States, a strong national movement is necessary for this purpose. For over a century the ruling elite has employed any possible means to colonize American minds. It has been quite successful in implanting in American mind the concept of capitalism as being good, democratic and necessary for happiness. Comparatively, the old territorial colonization was much easier to destroy than this mental one. Capitalism has become a deep seated belief in American mind like a religion. However with advance of electronic information technology, the activist movements are made incredibly easier and effective. There is a strong hope of success if **we the people** unite with determination to materialize technological democracy.

REFERENCES

The theory of technological democracy, which has been presented here in a simple form for general public, is a scientific theory and somehow complex, as any scientific theory, since it is based on logic and reasoning. That is one strong reason why it has taken three books by the author to present this immense societal theory in detail, to analyze with logic and reasoning each situation for proper understanding as well as appropriate implementation of it. And, that is also why the gradual and painstaking development of the theory has taken over thirty years of search, research, original thinking, and rethinking. Therefore, it is highly recommended that those who desire for a humanistic future society for their own country or the world, or determined to organize and take action for this purpose, read at least the first one of the three books and for additional enlightenment look into the other two. For the brief description of each book and how to acquire it see the author's website www.democracywhere.com also <www.Amazon.com> . Expression of thoughts and opinions are welcomed by the author which can be contacted at democrac@democracywhere.com For more materials about the subject in the form of articles see www.ezinearticles.com/ ?expert=Dr._Reza_Rezazadeh

Technological Democracy: A Humanistic Philosophy of the Future Society, 1990, 365 pp.

Technodemocratic Economic Theory: From Capitalism and Socialism to Democracy, 1991, 359 pp.

Passage to a Just Society: Secrets of Democratic Life, Leisure and Happiness, 2002, 294 pp.

SOME VALUABLE REFERENCES:

Amin, Samir. *Accumulation on a World Scale.* New York: Monthly Review Press, 1972.

Bell, Daniel. *The Coming of Post-industrial Society.* New York: Basic Books, 1973.

_____. *The Cultural Contradictions of Capitalism.* 2d ed. Exeter. New Hampshire: Heinmann Educational Books, 1979.

Bereano, Phillip L. *Technology as a Social and Political Phenomenon.* New York: Wilcy, 1979.

Blumberg, Paul. *Inequality in an Age of Decline.* New York: Oxford University Press, 1980.

Callenbach, Ernest. *Ecotopia.* New York: Bantam, 1977.

Cohen, Carl. *Communism, Fascism, and Democracy.* 2d ed. New York: Random House, 1972.

Conley, Patrick T. *Democracy in Decline.* Providence: Rhode Island Publications in Society, 1977.

Davis, Gregory H. *Technology: Humanism or Nihilism: A Critical Analysis of the Philosophical Basis and Practice of Modern Technology.* Lanham, Missouri: University Press of America, 1981.

Edmunds, Stahri W. *Alternate U.S. Futures.* Santa Monica, California: Goodyear, 1978.

Ellul, Jacques. *The Technological Society.* Translated by John Wilkinson. New York: Knopf, 1964.

Ferkiss, Victor. *The Future of Technological Civilization.* New York: Braziller, 1974.

Fromm, Erich. *Revolution of Hope: Toward a Humanized Technology.* New York: Harper and Row, 1974.

Calbraith, John K. *The New Industrial State.* 3rd ed. Boston: Haughton-Mifflin, 1978.

Hayek, Freidrich A. *Social Justice, Socialism and Democracy.* Terramurse, Australia: Center for Independent Studies, 1979.

Judson, H. F. *The Search for Solutions.* New York: Holt Rinehart and Winston, 1980.

Kozol, Jonathan. *Illiterate America.* Garden City, New York: Anchor Press/Doubleday, 1985.

Lindsay, A. D. *The Essentials of Democracy.* Oxford: Clarendon Press, 1929.

Miles, Rufus E., Jr. *Awakening from the American Dream: The Social and Political Limits to Growth.* New York: Universe Books, 1977.

Schumpeter, Joseph A. *Capitalism, Socialism, and Democracy.* New York: Harper and Row, 1950.

Schuster, Edward. *Human Rights Today: Evolution or Revolution.* New York: Philosophical Library, 1980.

Skinner, B. F. *Beyond Freedom and dignity.* New York: Bantam, 1972.

Toynbee, Arnold. *Mankind and Mother Earth.* New York: Oxford University Press, 1976.

Wilson, H. B. *Democracy and the Workplace.* Montreal, Canada: Black Rose Books, 1974.